BODY WORKS

Brilliant BRAIN

Anna Claybourne

QEB

QEB Publishing

Created for QEB Publishing by Tall Tree Ltd
Editor: Rob Colson
Designer: Jonathan Vipond
Illustrations, activities: Peter Bull
Illustrations, cartoons: Bill Greenhead

Copyright © QEB Publishing 2014

Project editor for QEB: Ruth Symons

First published in the United States by
QEB Publishing, Inc.
3 Wrigley, Suite A
Irvine, CA 92618

www.qed-publishing.co.uk

A CIP record for this book is available from the Library of Congress.

ISBN 978 1 60992 449 2

Printed in China

Picture credits
(t=top, b=bottom, l=left, r=right, c=center)
Alamy 13b Aflo Foto Agency **Getty** 25 AFP
Shutterstock 4b Monkey Business Images,
5b Mircea Bezergheanu, 6t leedsn, 6c Arteki,
6b Tischenko Irina, 7b naluwan, 13t Alex Mit,
14b michaeljung, 15t nobeastsofierce, 17t Fotokostic,
19b DenisNata, 21t DuleS, 21b takayuki, 22b Malyugin,
28t pryzmat, 28b Henrik Larsson, 29t Diego Barbieri
SPL 4-5, 20-21 Nancy Kedersha, 4t Volker Steger,
9 Chris Gallagher, 11 Sheila Terry, 23b Omikron

Note
In preparation of this book, all due care has been
exercised with regard to the activities and advice
depicted. The publishers regret that they can accept
no liability for any loss or injury sustained.

Words in **bold** are explained
in the Glossary on page 31.

CONTENTS

WHAT IS THE BRAIN?...4

EXPERIMENT: FIND YOUR DOMINANT SIDE..........6

THE THINKING BRAIN 8

ACTIVITY: THINKING CAP 10

THE BRAIN AND THE BODY 12

NERVE CELLS 14

SIGNALS AND REFLEXES 16

EXPERIMENT: TEST YOUR REACTIONS 18

LEARNING AND MEMORY 20

SENSES: SIGHT..22

SENSES: HEARING...24

SENSES: TASTE AND SMELL................................26

SENSES: TOUCH 28

EXPERIMENT: CONFUSE YOUR BRAIN 30

GLOSSARY 31

INDEX 32

WHAT IS THE BRAIN?

Your brain is your body's central HQ. It sorts out what you can see, hear, and feel, stores information, makes decisions, and sends out signals to control your body. It's basically a super powerful computer, squeezed inside your head!

A Brain of Two Halves

Your brain is divided into two **hemispheres**. Each is nearly a mirror-image of the other side. The right hemisphere controls the left-hand side of the body. The left hemisphere controls the right-hand side of the body. If you are right-handed, that means your left hemisphere is **dominant**.

YOUR BRAIN IS YOU!

Your brain is where you find your mind—what makes you who you are. Your personality and memories are saved in your brain. Skills such as playing football or being good at puzzles are also kept there.

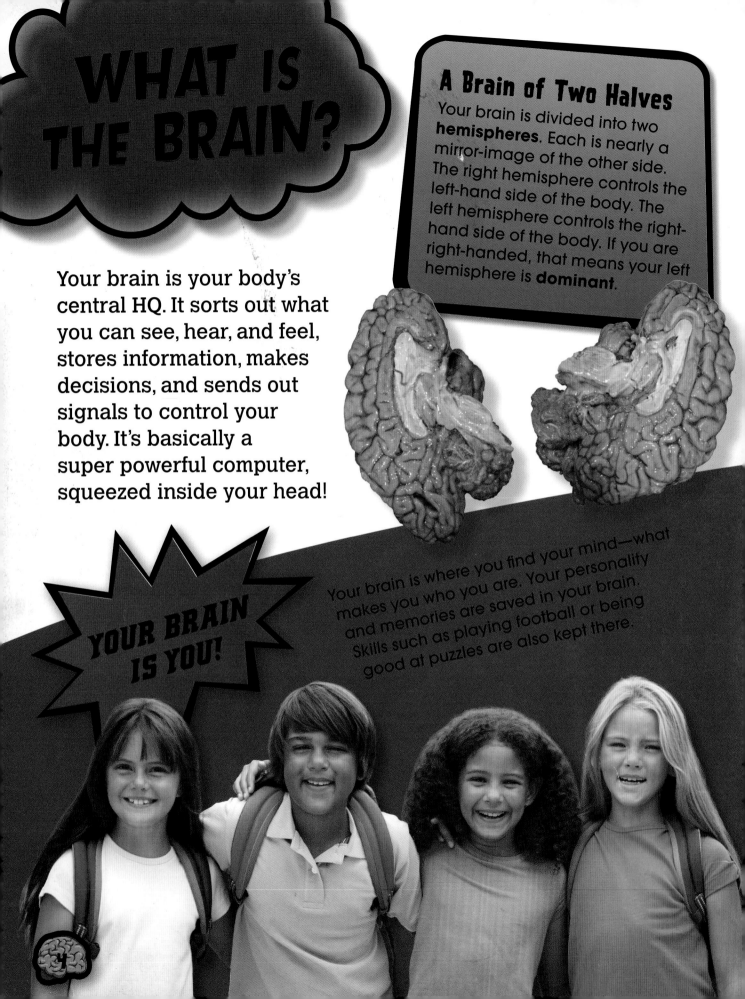

BRAIN PARTS

The **limbic system** is a cluster of parts in the middle of the brain that deals with memories and emotions.

The **corpus callosum** connects the two halves of the cerebrum.

The **cortex** is the wrinkly outer layer of the cerebrum, used for thinking.

The **cerebrum** is the biggest part of the brain.

The **brain stem** joins the brain to the spinal cord.

The **cerebellum** at the back of the brain helps control movement and balance.

IMAGINE THIS...

We couldn't live without our brains. But not every living thing has one. A starfish is completely brainless! It can survive without the need to think.

The **spinal cord** connects the brain to the rest of the body.

FIND YOUR DOMINANT SIDE

Most people have a dominant side—the side they use most for writing and other everyday tasks. Take these tests and write down the results to see which is your dominant side.

HANDS

1 Which hand do you use to write with?

2 Throw a small ball or beanbag up in the air. Which hand do you use?

3 When you use a computer, which hand do you move the mouse with?

FEET

1 Run on the spot for a few seconds, then jump into the air. Which foot did you push off from?

2 Drop a ball or beanbag, and kick it. Which foot did you use?

3 Put a coin on the ground, and step on it. Which foot did you use?

EYES

1 Hold your arms out in front of you, and make a triangle with your hands, like this.

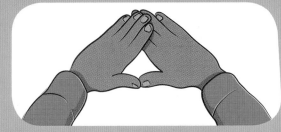

Move the triangle around until you can see a small object through the hole. Look at it with both eyes.

Now slowly bring the triangle closer and closer to your face, looking at the object all the time, until your hands are touching your face. Which eye did you bring them to?

2 Wink. Which eye did you keep open? This is probably your dominant one, since you keep your best eye open.

3 Hold an old paper towel tube up to your eye like a telescope. Which eye did you pick?

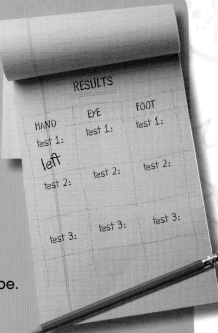

RESULTS

HAND	EYE	FOOT
test 1:	test 1:	test 1:
left		
test 2:	test 2:	test 2:
test 3:	test 3:	test 3:

What Happened?

Your results show you which side is dominant for each task. For most people, the same side is dominant in all the tests, but for some people, different sides are dominant in different tasks.

Left or Right?

For most people, the right side is dominant—but not for everyone. About 1 in 10 people are left-handed, 2 in 10 are left-footed, and 3 in 10 are left-eyed.

THE THINKING BRAIN

Use your brain! If anyone's ever said that to you, they were probably telling you to THINK. We all know the brain is used for thinking. But how it actually does this is a bit of a mystery.

FRONT

Muscle control

Touch

Planning movement

Long-term planning

Speaking

Taste

Hearing

Smell

CORTEX CONTROL

The cortex is the wrinkly outer layer of the brain. It is where most of our thinking takes place. It's sometimes called "gray matter" because of its color. Different parts of the cortex deal with different things.

FRONTAL LOBE

The most important part of the cortex for thinking is a part called the **frontal lobe**. It is right at the front of your brain, tucked away behind your forehead. This is where you think about whether something is a good or a bad idea. Your frontal lobe can keep you out of trouble!

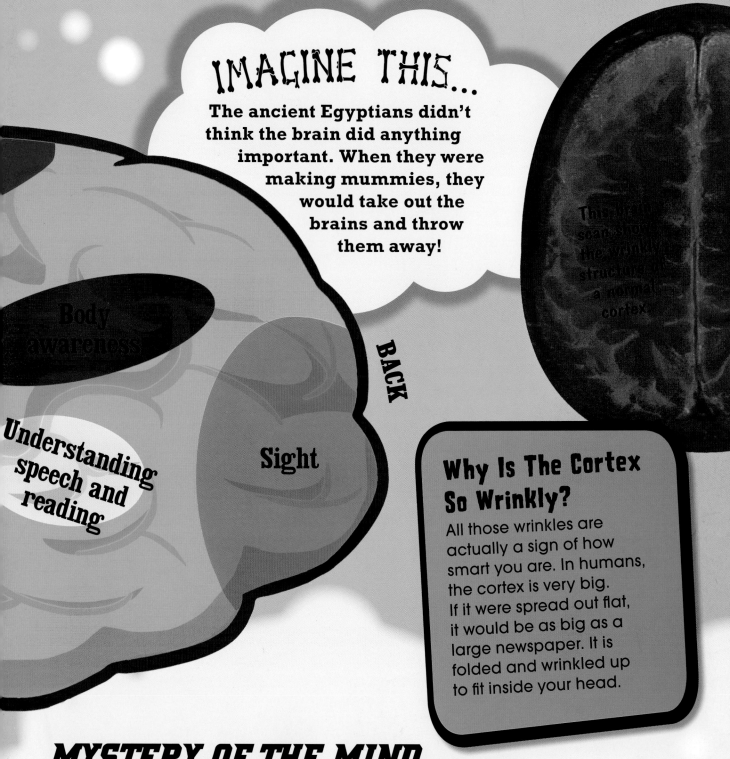

IMAGINE THIS...

The ancient Egyptians didn't think the brain did anything important. When they were making mummies, they would take out the brains and throw them away!

Body awareness

Understanding speech and reading

Sight

BACK

This brain scan shows the wrinkly structure of a normal cortex.

Why Is The Cortex So Wrinkly?

All those wrinkles are actually a sign of how smart you are. In humans, the cortex is very big. If it were spread out flat, it would be as big as a large newspaper. It is folded and wrinkled up to fit inside your head.

MYSTERY OF THE MIND...

Scientists know we use our brains for thinking. But how is it that we know we're thinking? How does the brain create a picture in your "mind's eye?" How can it come up with a brilliant idea, or make you feel jealous, or help you write a poem? Being aware of who we are and what we feel is called being **conscious**, and we still don't really know how that works.

THINKING CAP

Show off your colorful cortex with this papier-mâché hat.

YOU WILL NEED:

- Water
- White glue
- Clean, empty, small yogurt cup or food carton
- Popsicle stick or spoon for stirring
- Large bowl or clean, empty food carton
- Old newspaper
- Large balloon
- Scissors
- Pens, paints, and paintbrushes

1 In the bowl, mix two yogurt cups of glue with one of water. Stir well.

2 Tear the newspaper into small strips or pieces.

3 Blow up the balloon until it is slightly bigger than your head. Tie a knot in it.

4 One by one, dip the pieces of newspaper into the glue mixture, and lay them onto the balloon, overlapping each other. Keep going until you have covered the top half of the balloon, then leave to dry. Add two more layers of paper in the same way.

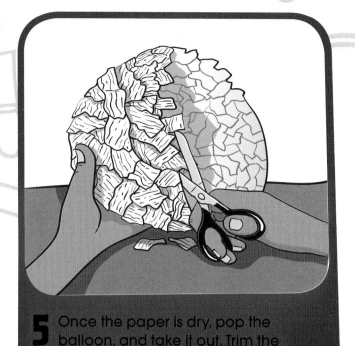

5 Once the paper is dry, pop the balloon, and take it out. Trim the edges of the cap with scissors, paint it white and leave it to dry.

6 Finally, decorate the cap with the different areas of the cortex, as shown on page 8. Mark the areas with a black pen, fill them in with different colors and add labels saying what each part does.

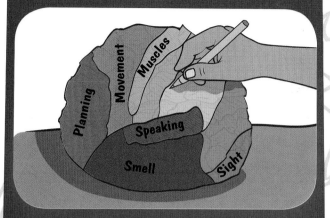

For a different version, you could decorate your cap to look pink and wrinkly, like a real brain.

Different areas of the skull were once thought to indicate different qualities, such as kindness or honesty. The areas are illustrated here with pictures.

LUMPS AND BUMPS

In the 1800s, many scientists thought that lumps and bumps on your head revealed the shape of your brain. They thought that this showed whether you were a good or bad person! Now we know that whatever kind of brain you have, it doesn't change the shape of your skull.

THE BRAIN AND THE BODY

Your brain is linked to every part of your body by a network of pathways called **nerves**. Nerves allow the brain to stay in touch with your senses and control your actions. Together, the brain and nerves make up the **nervous system**.

The brain and spinal cord are known as the central nervous system. The rest of the nerves are called the peripheral nervous system.

NERVOUS NETWORK

A big bundle of nerves—the spinal cord—leads out of your brain stem and down your back. Nerve pathways branch off from the spinal cord. They lead to your arms and fingers, legs and toes, muscles, joints, and **organs** such as the heart. Nerves also connect to your sense organs—the eyes, ears, nose, tongue, and skin.

Brain stem

Spinal cord

Nerves

SPINE HIGHWAY

The spinal cord acts like a main road for your nervous system's messages. It runs down your neck and back inside your backbone, or spine, which protects it from knocks. If you break your back, you may become paralyzed, meaning that you cannot move. This is because signals to and from your body cannot get through.

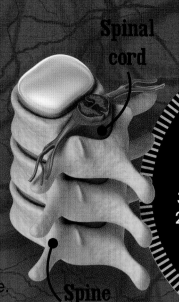

Spinal cord

Spine

HOW FAST?

Nerve signals travel quickly! A message whizzing from your hand to your brain can go as fast as 300 feet per second. That's 230 mph (370 km/h)—faster than a speeding train.

ZOOMING SIGNALS

Signals from the senses zoom along the nerves to the brain to tell it what's going on, for example, the fact that a ball is coming toward you. Inside the brain, signals whiz around as you process the information. Then the brain sends signals along the nerves to the body to tell it what action to take, such as "catch the ball!"

The eyes see the ball and send a signal to the brain.

The brain sends signals to the arm and hand to catch the ball.

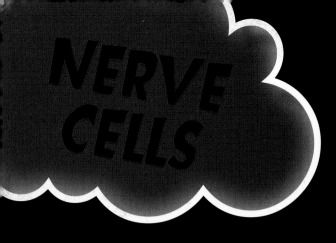

NERVE CELLS

The body is made up of tiny units called **cells**. The cells in the brain and nervous system are called nerve cells, or **neurons**. They carry signals between the brain and the body. Neurons also send messages to each other. This allows the brain to solve difficult problems.

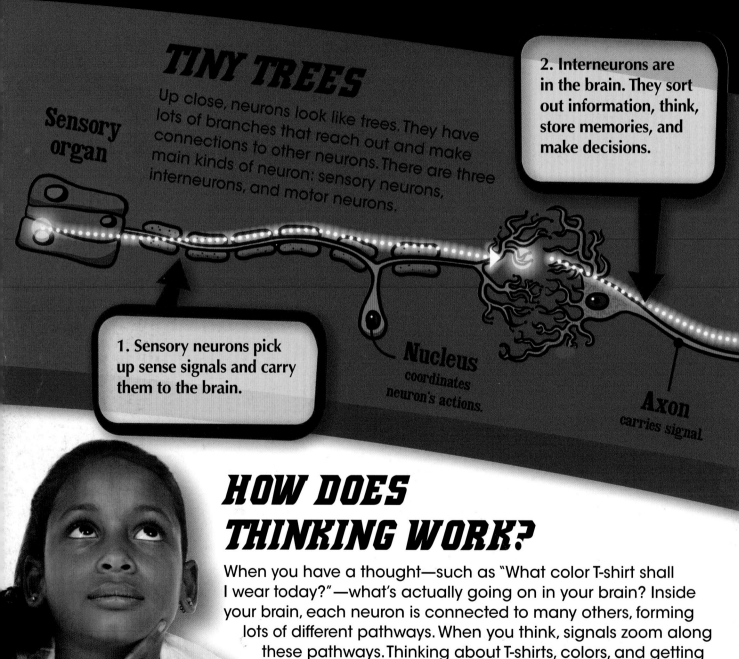

TINY TREES

Up close, neurons look like trees. They have lots of branches that reach out and make connections to other neurons. There are three main kinds of neuron: sensory neurons, interneurons, and motor neurons.

2. Interneurons are in the brain. They sort out information, think, store memories, and make decisions.

Sensory organ

1. Sensory neurons pick up sense signals and carry them to the brain.

Nucleus
coordinates neuron's actions.

Axon
carries signal

HOW DOES THINKING WORK?

When you have a thought—such as "What color T-shirt shall I wear today?"—what's actually going on in your brain? Inside your brain, each neuron is connected to many others, forming lots of different pathways. When you think, signals zoom along these pathways. Thinking about T-shirts, colors, and getting dressed will activate several different pathways.

SIZZLING SYNAPSES

Signals travel along a neuron as a tiny flow of electricity. Where one neuron connects to the next, there's a small gap, called a **synapse**. To carry the signal across a synapse, the neuron releases chemicals that the next neuron picks up.

Chemicals pass across the synaptic gap, allowing messages to pass between neurons.

Dendrites pick up signals from other neurons.

Nucleus

Myelin sheath protects the axon.

Muscle

IMAGINE THIS...

The brain contains around 100 BILLION neurons. Each neuron can link to more than a thousand others. That means there are trillions of connections and possible pathways— and thoughts!

3. Motor neurons carry instructions from the brain to the muscles.

15

When messages reach your brain from your senses, you need to act on them! You might want to move your foot to kick a ball, or turn your head when someone calls your name.

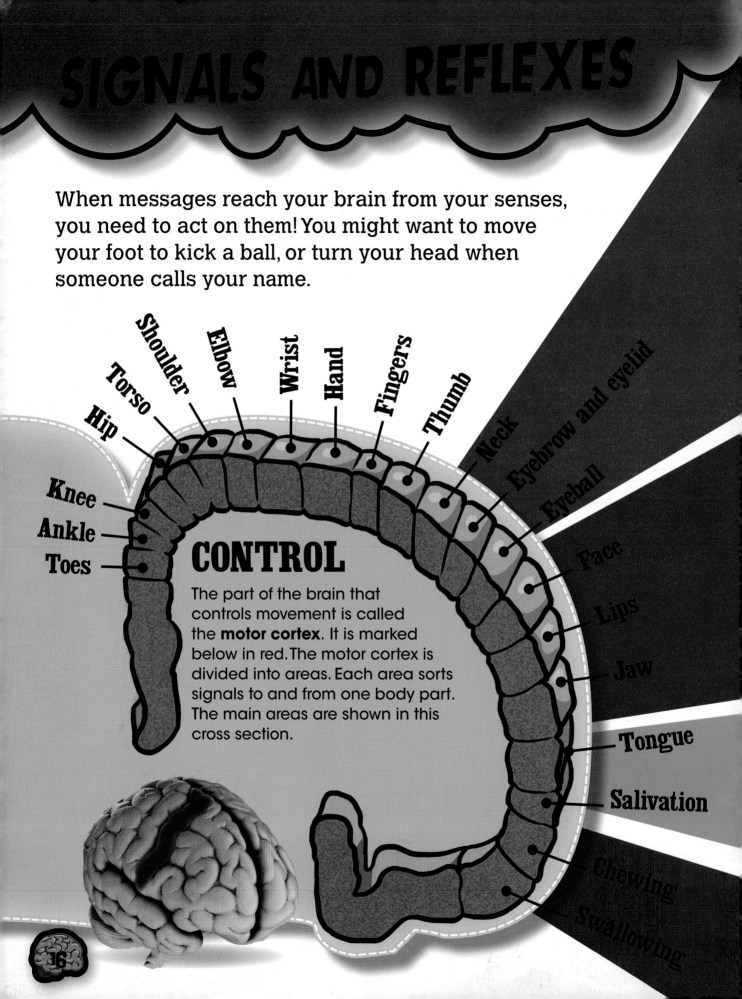

Shoulder
Elbow
Torso
Wrist
Hand
Hip
Fingers
Thumb
Neck
Eyebrow and eyelid
Eyeball
Knee
Face
Ankle
Toes
Lips
Jaw
Tongue
Salivation
Chewing
Swallowing

CONTROL

The part of the brain that controls movement is called the **motor cortex**. It is marked below in red. The motor cortex is divided into areas. Each area sorts signals to and from one body part. The main areas are shown in this cross section.

REFLEX REACTIONS

If you accidentally touch a hot pan, you jerk your hand away almost immediately. This reaction is called a reflex, and it doesn't need the brain. Instead, a danger signal travels to the spinal cord, which sends signals straight to the muscles. This saves precious time.

MOTOR MAYHEM

Drugs such as alcohol slow down brain signals and make them less accurate. That's why drinking alcohol can make people dizzy and clumsy.

For complicated activities, such as playing soccer, several parts of the motor cortex are sending signals at once.

What's That?

This is a homunculus—a model of the body. In this homunculus, each body part is sized according to how much of the motor cortex is used to control it. The hands are huge as they make very complex movements that need lots of brain power to get right.

TEST YOUR REACTIONS

CATCH IT!

It is difficult to measure reaction times, since your brain and body work so fast. This experiment uses the markings on a ruler to find out how fast you are.

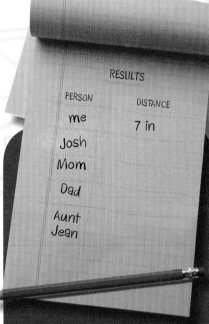

RESULTS	
PERSON	DISTANCE
me	7 in
Josh	
Mom	
Dad	
Aunt Jean	

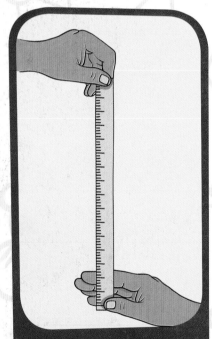

1 Get someone to hold the ruler upright, with 0 at the bottom end and 12 in (30 cm) at the top. Hold your thumb and finger apart, level with the bottom of the ruler.

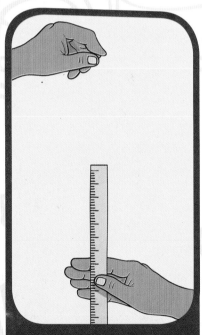

2 The other person lets go of the ruler, and you have to grab it as soon as you see it start to fall.

3 The number where your fingers grab the ruler is your score. The lower it is, the faster your nervous system! Ask friends and family to try it, too, and see who is fastest.

Try the same test, but use your non-dominant hand. Is it slower?

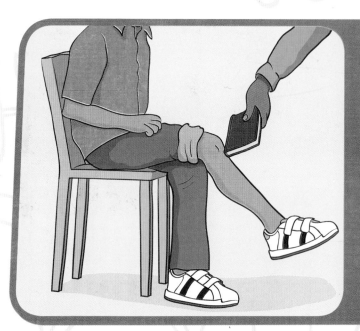

KNEE-JERK!

Sit with your legs crossed like this. Ask someone to tap your upper knee sharply, just below the kneecap, with the edge of the notebook.

Knee-jerk! Your knee kicks when it's tapped. It's part of the **proprioception** system that helps you balance (see page 29). The spinal cord controls this reflex.

DON'T BLINK!

Stand behind a window or clear glass door, with your face up against the glass. Ask someone to throw cotton balls at your face. Your challenge is to keep your eyes open. Can you do it?

Even though you know you're behind glass, your body has a reflex that shuts your eyes—so it's really hard not to blink! This reflex protects the eyes when something flies toward them.

Staying Alert

Try the tests after breakfast when you feel wide awake, and at bedtime when you're sleepy. Is there a difference in your results?

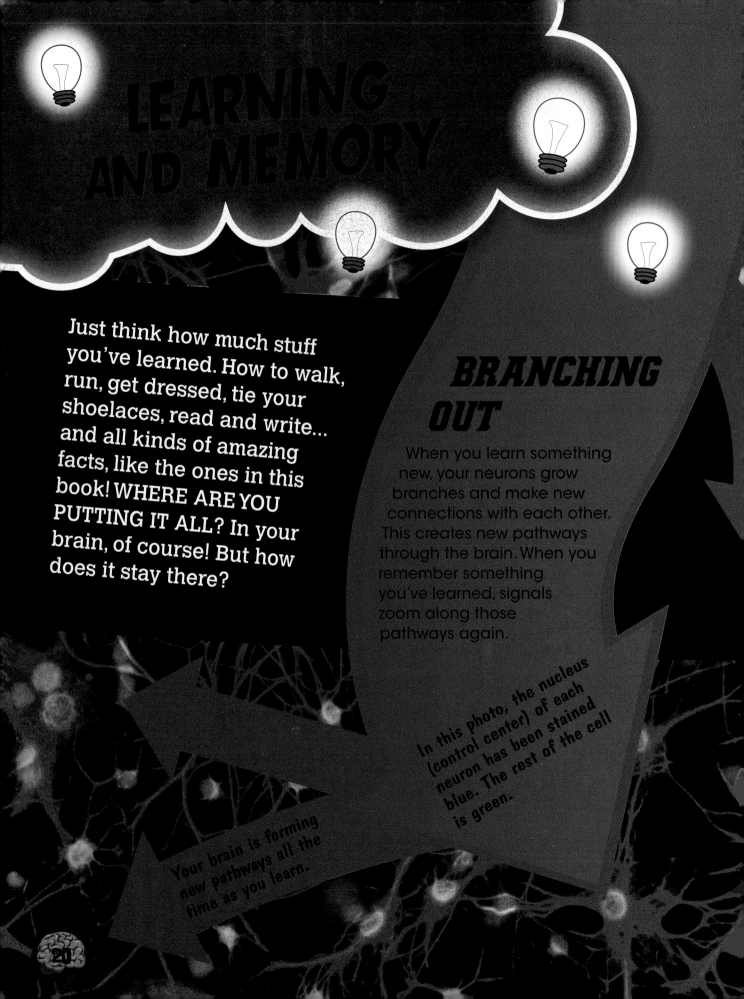

LEARNING AND MEMORY

Just think how much stuff you've learned. How to walk, run, get dressed, tie your shoelaces, read and write... and all kinds of amazing facts, like the ones in this book! WHERE ARE YOU PUTTING IT ALL? In your brain, of course! But how does it stay there?

BRANCHING OUT

When you learn something new, your neurons grow branches and make new connections with each other. This creates new pathways through the brain. When you remember something you've learned, signals zoom along those pathways again.

In this photo, the nucleus (control center) of each neuron has been stained blue. The rest of the cell is green.

Your brain is forming new pathways all the time as you learn.

It's On the Tip of My Tongue!

Everyone has moments when they can't remember a word or name, even though they know they know it. This is called Tip-Of-Tongue, or TOT, syndrome. Memory isn't perfect, and things can get mixed up or are remembered very weakly. We forget them or have to struggle to "find" them.

GROWING BRAINS

Your brain is constantly building new connections as you learn more about the world. The pathways that are used the most become stronger and more fixed. Those that are used least fade away.

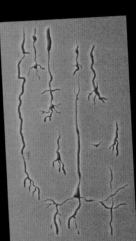

Connections at birth

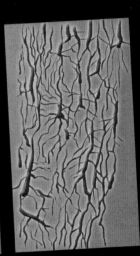

Connections age 6

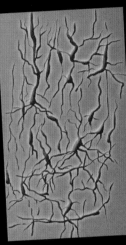

Connections age 14

ZZZZZZZZZZZZZ!

Sleep is very important for your brain. When you sleep, the brain sorts through what you've experienced and learned that day. Some things get laid down as memories; others are deleted. This frees up your brain to think and take in new stuff the next day.

Most people spend a third of their lives asleep!

Your senses are your brain's window on the world. When you have your eyes open, they send a stream of nerve signals, which the brain uses to create a picture of the world around you.

SEEING THE LIGHT

By sensing the light that bounces off objects, we get a good idea of where we are and what's around us. Sight is one of our most useful senses (though people can manage without it).

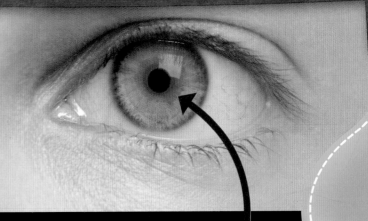

LETTING IN LIGHT

Go into a dimly lit room and look in a mirror. Then switch on a light. You should see your pupils suddenly shrink. This is a reflex reaction (see page 17). When it's dark, your pupils open wide to collect all the light they can. In bright light, they shrink to protect the eye. The size of the pupil is controlled by the iris—the colored part of the eye.

Your pupil quickly shrinks when a light is turned on.

As light from an object enters the eye, it makes an image on your **retina** that is actually upside down and back to front. Your brain flips the picture back so that when you "see" it in your head, it makes sense.

It's a tree!

4. The brain compares the image to its memory banks to figure out what you are seeing.

Cornea

Retina

3. Light-detecting neurons sense the light and send signals to the brain.

Water-filled chamber

Optic nerve

1. Light rays from objects pass through the pupil in the front of the eye. The light is focused by a lens.

2. The light rays make an upside-down image of the object on the retina at the back of the eyeball.

Here, the rods are green, and the cones are blue.

RODS AND CONES

The retina is made up of two different types of light sensor, called rods and cones. Cones detect colors. Rods are more sensitive than cones and help us see in darker conditions. Rods cannot detect colors, which is why we see in black and white at night.

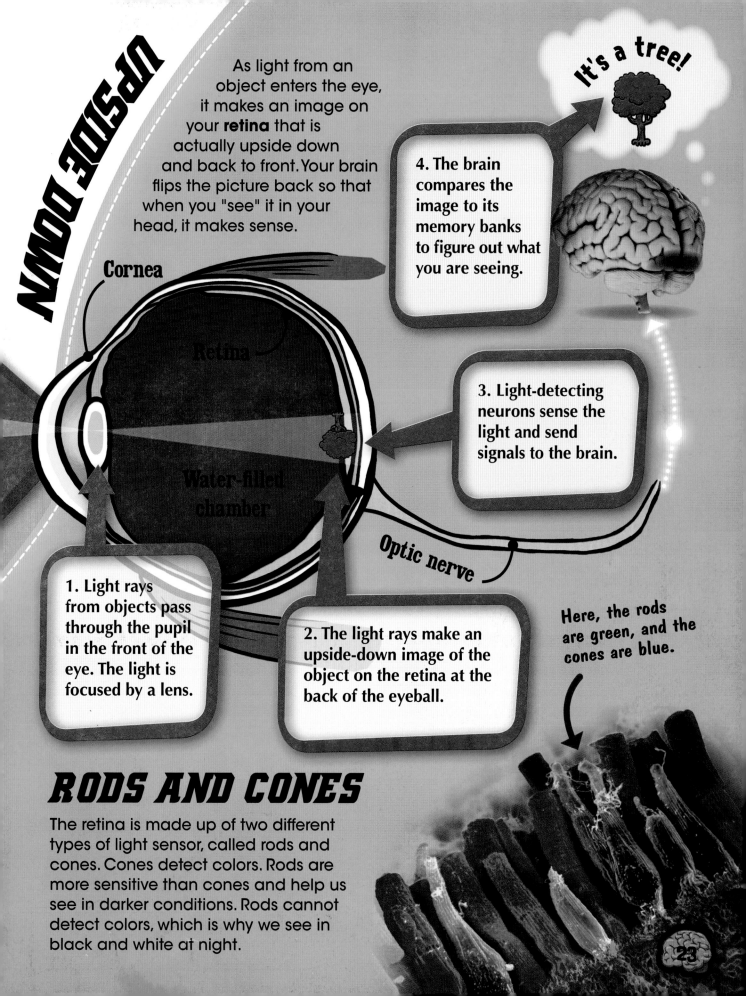

SENSES: HEARING

Sounds are vibrations in the air caused by the movement of objects. To detect these vibrations, your ears contain eardrums—little disks of tightly stretched skin. When vibrating air enters your ears, it makes your eardrums vibrate, too.

Pinna
funnels sounds into ear canal

HOW YOUR EARS WORK

1. Sound vibrations enter the ear and travel along the ear canal to the eardrum, making it vibrate.

Ear canal

Outer ear

GOING IN...

Ears aren't just on the outside of your body—they are complex organs that reach deep into the sides of your head.

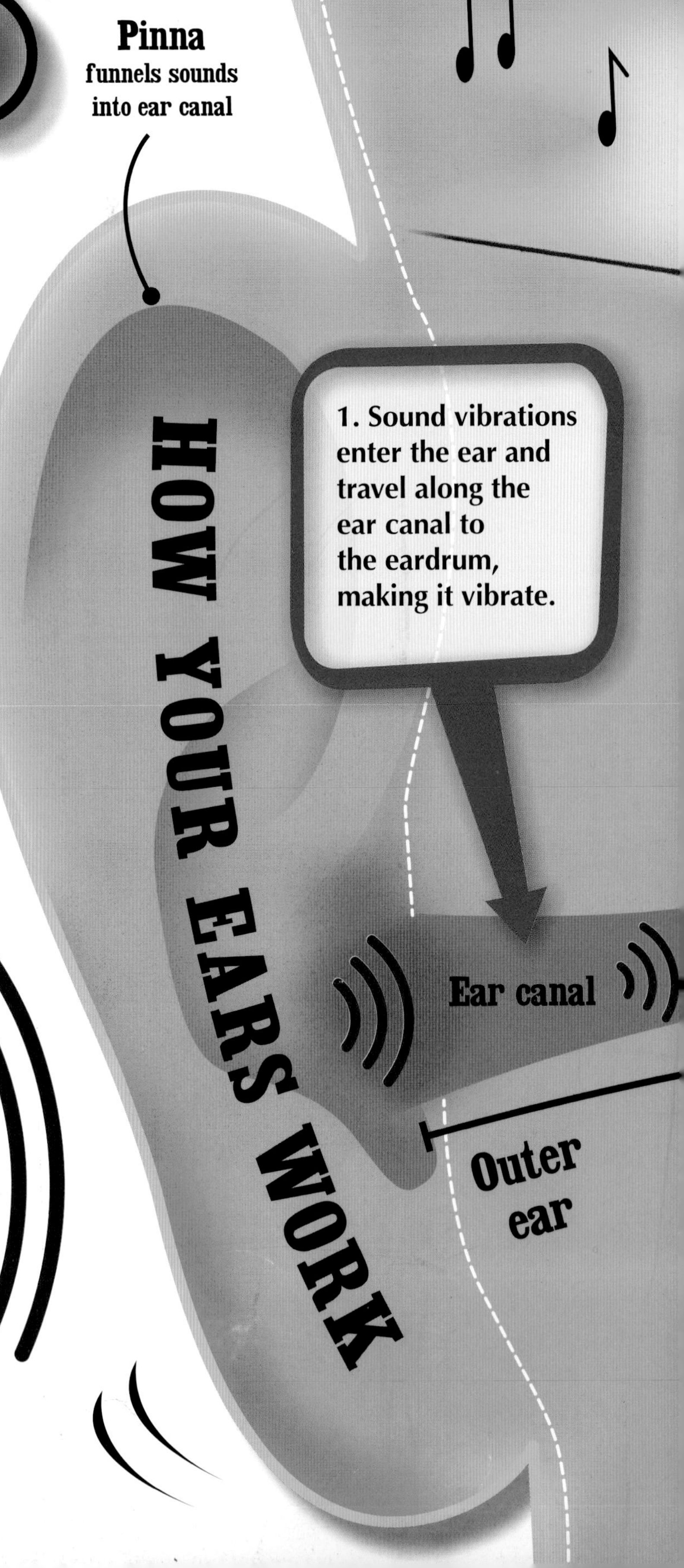

DON'T FALL DOWN!

Besides sensing sound vibrations, the ear does another important job. It helps you keep your balance. Parts called the semicircular canals contain a liquid. When your head tilts, the liquid moves. Sensitive hairs pick up this movement and send signals to your brain. This means you keep track of which way up you are.

Semicircular canals

Anvil

Hammer

5. The brain decodes the vibration patterns into meaningful sounds.

Cochlea

Stirrup

Nerve leading into brain

Eardrum

Middle ear

Inner ear

2. The vibrations pass through a series of bones inside the ear, called the hammer, anvil, and stirrup (so-called because of their shapes).

3. The vibrations spread into a spiral-shaped part called the cochlea, deep inside the ear.

4. Sensory neurons attached to tiny hairs in the cochlea detect the vibrations and send signals to the brain.

23

SENSES: TASTE AND SMELL

Food is essential for your body, but it's bad news if you eat something poisonous or rotten. The senses of taste and smell help the brain figure out if food is good or bad.

SMELL

Sniff, sniff! Whenever you take a good sniff of something, tiny bits of that substance float straight up inside your nose. Your nose sends signals to your brain to tell it what you're smelling.

Signals are sent from smell receptors to the olfactory bulb at the front of the brain.

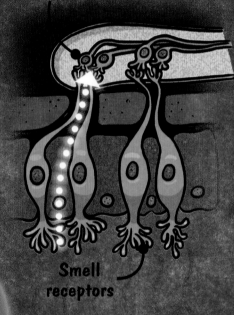

Olfactory bulb

Smell receptors

SMELL

IMAGINE THIS...

Dogs' noses are very sensitive, with up to 50 times more smell receptors than a human nose. A dog's nose is covered in a gooey liquid called mucus. The mucus helps the dog smell by capturing scent particles from the air.

TASTE

Tastes are detected by taste buds on your tongue. They detect just five tastes: salt, sweet, sour, bitter, and umami (savory). Some of your food also wafts up to your smell detectors. So the taste of food is actually a mixture of tastes and smells.

For you to taste food, it has to be dissolved in saliva (spit) and washed down into pores (gaps) in the surface of your tongue. The tiny taste buds are found in these gaps.

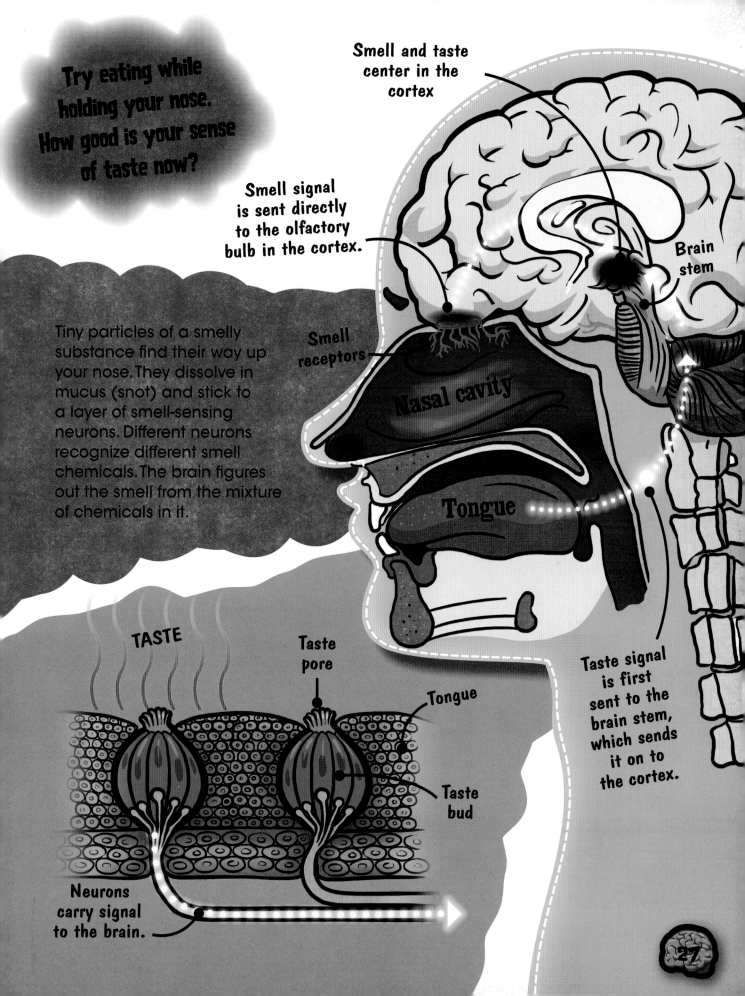

Try eating while holding your nose. How good is your sense of taste now?

Smell and taste center in the cortex

Smell signal is sent directly to the olfactory bulb in the cortex.

Brain stem

Smell receptors

Tiny particles of a smelly substance find their way up your nose. They dissolve in mucus (snot) and stick to a layer of smell-sensing neurons. Different neurons recognize different smell chemicals. The brain figures out the smell from the mixture of chemicals in it.

Nasal cavity

Tongue

Taste signal is first sent to the brain stem, which sends it on to the cortex.

TASTE

Taste pore

Tongue

Taste bud

Neurons carry signal to the brain.

27

SENSES: TOUCH

Your skin keeps you warm, protects you, and holds all your body parts together. But it also has another important job. It's stuffed with tiny touch detectors—neurons that send signals to your brain about what you can feel.

BRAILLE

The sense of touch is especially useful for people who can't see. Braille is a code of raised dots that can be felt with the fingertips. It allows blind people to read books.

THIS FEELS FUNNY!

Your fingers can tell you whether an object is warm or cool, solid or squishy, smooth, scratchy, furry, spiky, wet, or dry. This is because your skin contains several different types of sensory neurons. They detect heat, cold, and pressure. They also sense damage to your skin, which your brain experiences as pain.

An insect bite is felt as a sharp pain.

IMAGINE THIS...

Imagine you had to have an arm or leg amputated, but after it was gone ...you could STILL FEEL IT! This really happens, and it's called a phantom limb. The brain acts as if the limb were still there. It takes time to adapt to the change.

Hair lies flat

muscle relaxes

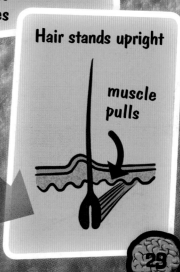

Hair stands upright

muscle pulls

GOOSE BUMPS?

You get goose bumps when you're cold or scared. Tiny muscles pull on your hairs and make them stand upright. In furry animals, this traps air close to the skin, helping them stay warm. It can also make them look bigger—useful for putting off predators. But most of our hairs are tiny, so goose bumps aren't very effective. Brrrrrr!

CONFUSE YOUR BRAIN

Your brain is constantly dealing with signals from your senses. Sometimes it makes mistakes or gets mixed up. Here are some ways to bamboozle your poor brain...

1 Are the horizontal lines straight or not?

They are straight! The pattern of black blocks and gray lines confuses the brain and makes the lines seem to tilt and slope.

2 How many triangles can you see?

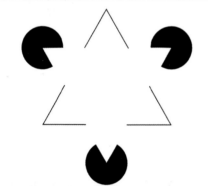

There aren't any triangles in the picture, but the other shapes make your brain "fill in" a triangle shape.

3 Which person is the biggest?

They're all the same size! The figures appear with perspective lines that make the top one look like he is farther away. Your brain knows that objects appear smaller when they are farther away, so it assumes the top figure must be bigger than he appears.

What Is Going On?

To save time, your brain makes guesses based on what it has experienced before. These guesses can sometimes be wrong, which causes optical illusions like these.

30

GLOSSARY

BRAIN STEM
Lowest section of the brain. It connects the brain to the rest of the body.

CELLS
The tiny units that all living things are made of.

CEREBELLUM
Area at the back of the brain, used for moving and balancing.

CEREBRUM
The largest section of the brain, which looks like a giant walnut.

CONSCIOUS
Aware of yourself and your own thoughts and feelings.

CORPUS CALLOSUM
Bundle of fibers connecting the two halves of the brain together.

CORTEX
The wrinkled outer layer of the brain, used for thinking and understanding.

DOMINANT
Strong and controlling. The dominant side of the brain controls complex tasks.

FRONTAL LOBE
Front part of the brain, where calculating and decision-making happen.

HEMISPHERE
One half of the brain. The brain contains a left and right hemisphere.

LIMBIC SYSTEM
Section of the brain that deals with emotions, memories, and urges.

MOTOR CORTEX
Part of the brain that controls movement.

NERVE
A neuron or bundle of neurons that carries signals around the brain and body.

NERVOUS SYSTEM
The brain and the nerves that connect it to different parts of the body.

NEURONS
The cells that make up the brain and nervous system.

ORGAN
A body part that does a particular job, such as the brain, heart, or stomach.

PROPRIOCEPTION
Type of touch sense that tells the brain how the body is positioned.

RETINA
The layer of light-detecting cells at the back of the eyeball.

SPINAL CORD
Bundle of nerves leading from the brain stem down the middle of the back.

SYNAPSE
A tiny gap where signals jump from one neuron to the next.

INDEX

alcohol 17
ancient Egyptians 9
anvil 25
axon 14, 15

backbone 13
Braille 28
brain stem 5, 12, 27, 31

cell 14, 20, 31
cerebellum 5, 31
cerebrum 5, 31
cochlea 25
cones 23
connections 14, 15,
    20–21
conscious 9, 31
cornea 23
corpus callosum 5, 31
cortex 5, 8, 9, 10–11,
    27, 31

dendrite 15
dominant side 4, 6–7,
    31

ear 12, 24–25
eardrum 24, 25
eye 7, 12, 19, 22–23
eyeball 23

frontal lobe 8, 31

goose bumps 29
gray matter 8

hammer 25
hemisphere 4, 31
homunculus 17

interneuron 14
iris 22

limbic system 5, 31

memory 20–21, 23
motor cortex 16–17, 31
motor neuron 14–15
mummies 9
muscle 8, 12, 15
myelin sheath 15

nasal cavity 27
nerve 12–13, 25, 31
    cells 14–15
    optic nerve 23
    signals 22
nervous system 12, 18, 31
    central 12
    peripheral 12
neuron 14–15, 20, 31
nose 26–27
nucleus 14, 20

olfactory bulb 26
optic nerve 23
optical illusions 30
organ 12, 24, 31
    sensory 14

pathways 12, 15, 20–21
perspective lines 30
phantom limb 29
proprioception 19, 29, 31
pupil 22

reaction 17, 18–19,
    22
reflex 17, 18–19, 22
retina 23, 31
rods 23

saliva 26
semicircular canals 25
senses 12, 13, 16, 22–23,
    24–25, 26–27, 28–29, 30
sensory neuron 14–15, 25,
    28
sensory organ 14
sight 9, 22–23
signals 4, 13, 14, 16
sleep 21
sound 24–25
smell 26–27
smell receptors 26–27
spinal cord 5, 12–13, 17,
    19, 31
spine 13
stirrup 25
synapse 15, 31
synaptic gap 15

taste 26–27
taste bud 26–27
thinking 5, 8–9, 14, 31
Tip-Of-Tongue syndrome
    21
tongue 26, 27
touch 28–29

vibration 24–25